MONSTROUS MANNERS

MANNERS WITH TECHNOLOGY

BY BRIDGET HEOS  ILLUSTRATED BY KATYA LONGHI

Amicus Illustrated is published by Amicus
P.O. Box 1329, Mankato, MN 56002
www.amicuspublishing.us

Library of Congress Cataloging-in-Publication Data
Heos, Bridget, author.
 Manners with technology / by Bridget Heos;
Illustrated by Katya Longhi.
     pages cm. — (Amicus illustrated)
(Monstrous manners)
 Summary: "A young monster who takes her
sister's tablet computer without asking gets a
lesson in online etiquette and appropriate use of
electronics"— Provided by publisher.
 Audience: K to grade 3.
 ISBN 978-1-60753-748-9 (library binding) —
 ISBN 978-1-60753-847-9 (ebook)
1. Online etiquette—Juvenile literature. 2. Etiquette
for children and teenagers—Juvenile literature.
I. Longhi, Katya, illustrator. II. Title.
 TK5105.878.H46 2016
 395.5—dc23   2014041499

Editor: Rebecca Glaser
Designer: Kathleen Petelinsek

Printed in the United States of America at
Corporate Graphics in North Mankato, Minnesota.

10 9 8 7 6 5 4 3 2 1

ABOUT THE AUTHOR

Bridget Heos is the author of more than
70 books for children, including *Mustache
Baby* and *Mustache Baby Meets His Match*.
Her favorite manners are holding the door
for others and jumping up to help. You can
find out more about her, if you please, at
www.authorbridgetheos.com.

ABOUT THE ILLUSTRATOR

Katya Longhi was born in southern Italy.
She studied illustration at the Nemo
NT Academy of Digital Arts in Florence.
She loves to create dream worlds with
horses, flying dogs, and princesses in
her illustrations. She currently lives in
northern Italy with her Prince Charming.

Hey, that's my tablet, Monster! You need to ask before you use it. You can borrow it, but you'll need to learn some manners first.

Manners online are like manners with people. Be kind. If you wouldn't say something in person, don't send the message online, either.

Let's try it. Text a friend. That's very nice, Monster!

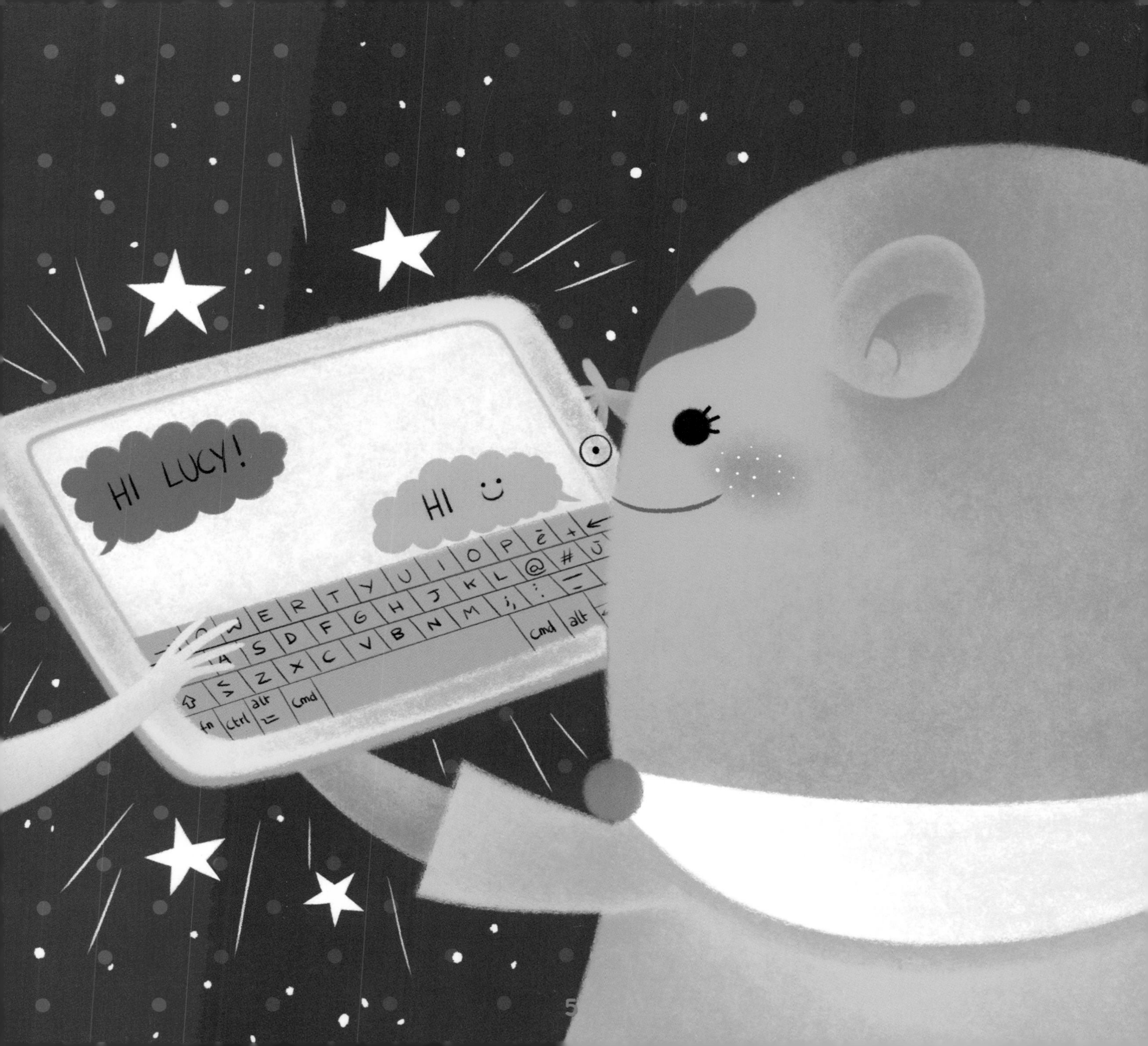
HI LUCY!
HI

Now, let's say you're watching a video and want to comment. Monster, that's mean.

But it will still hurt their feelings. Even if you use
a nickname to comment, you must be polite.

Now, let's say you're on a
website that lets you share
pictures. Grown-ups call this
"social media." Here's a funny
picture my friend Kevin posted.
What should I say?

Monster, I know it's a silly photo. But online, people can't see that you are smiling. So funny things can sound mean instead. Let's not post that comment.

Hey, what are you doing? Ugh. That's an awful picture! Don't post it online. Never share embarrassing photos. And don't post photos of other people without their permission, either.

That's my friend Laney calling to video chat.
Hi, Laney. Monster, making faces is not polite!

Instead of being silly, ask a question.
Then when you're done talking, say goodbye.

Look, Monster, your friend Lucy is here. Don't ignore her. When you're with friends, focus on them, and not your tablet or handheld game, okay?

If you play video games with friends, take turns. Or play a game where you both play at the same time.

Don't play for too long. Too much screen time can turn you into a zombie! And be sure to quit playing when a grown-up asks. Remember, Mom and Dad said we have a one-hour limit for video games.

Fresh air makes you feel good. And when you feel good,
you have better manners—whether in person or online.

See, that was good manners, Monster!

Look, Monster. It's an email from Grandma. Be sure to answer emails from friends and family! (But not strangers, of course.)

Check for spelling and grammar. That way, the email will be easier for Grandma to read. And she'll know that you put time and effort into it.

Wow! Good job knowing that, Monst—hey, you're
not a monster. You're my little sister Willow. Good
job learning your technology manners, Willow!

GOOD MANNERS WITH TECHNOLOGY

1. Ask before using someone else's phone, tablet, or computer.
2. Be kind to people online. Don't say mean things.
3. Ask before posting pictures of people online. Don't post embarrassing photos.
4. Don't make faces at people while video chatting.
5. Don't use phones, tablets, or games while talking with people in person. It will look like you're ignoring them.
6. Take turns when playing electronic games.
7. Respect the technology time limits that grown-ups have set.
8. Respond to emails from friends and family.
9. Check your spelling and grammar so that your email is clear to the person reading it.
10. Don't use phones, tablets, or games while eating meals.

READ MORE

Cornwall, Phyllis. *Mind Your Manners Online*. Ann Arbor, Mich.: Cherry Lake Publishing, 2012.

Heos, Bridget. *Be Safe on the Internet*. Mankato, Minn.: Amicus, 2015.

Ingalls, Ann. *Good Manners on the Phone*. Mankato, Minn.: The Child's World, 2013.

Miller, Shannon. *Be Nice Online*. New York: PowerKids Press, 2014.

WEBSITES

BrainPOP | Digital Etiquette
www.brainpop.com/technology/ computersandinternet/digitaletiquette/
Watch a video about digital etiquette— how to behave when you're on websites, email, chat rooms, and more.

Can You Teach My Alligator Manners?
disneyjunior.com/can-you-teach-my- alligator-manners
Watch videos and do activities to learn about manners in all different places, including restaurants, school, and more.

Learn about Manners:
Crafts and Activities for Kids
www.dltk-kids.com/crafts/ miscellaneous/manners.htm
Try these songs, crafts, and coloring pages to learn and practice good manners.